# GOOGLE DOCs ULTIMATE USER'S GUIDE

### Beginners illustrative Guide to Google Docs

## CHARLES

# DERRICK

# Copyright



Printed in the United States of America
© 2021 by Charles Derrick

**Table of Contents**

# Chapter 3 .................................................. 28

# Working with Tables in Google Docs .. 28



# Chapter 4 .................................................. 41

# Images, page numbers & graph ........... 41

# Chapter 5 .................................................50

# Making Bullet & Number Lists .............50



# Chapter 6 .................................................55

# Advanced Formatting and Page setup ...55



# Chapter 7 .................................................63

# Paragraph Styles in Google Docs ..........63

# Why This Guide?

If you have been thinking of getting a cloud-based document application package that enables you to type, format, edit and save your work, then Google Docs is  a good choice. Google  docs also enable  you to publish and print your document online. However, if you need  a comprehensive and  self-explanatory guide to walk you through how to use Google Docs, this guide  is the right  choice. In this  book, you  will be taken  through step-by-step practical illustrations with over  100 screenshots  on how  to  use the powerful App to  enable you  get the best  out of it. In fact, with  this guide, you  can do it  yourself.

# About the Author

Charles Derrick is a lover of tech with a wealth of experience in the ICT industry. Charles is a passionate follower of the latest technology and loves to proffer solution to complex problems. He is a Bachelor and Master's degree holder in Computer Science and Information Technology, respectively, from MIT, Boston, Massachusetts.

# Chapter 1

# Google Docs Basics

Google Doc is free cloud-based document application software in Google Drive used to type, format, edit, and save the document in Google Drive. It is similar to Microsoft Word in Microsoft Office. Google Doc has formatting toolbar and menu bar almost the same as that of Microsoft Word.

## How to Access Google Docs

To access Google Docs, follow the steps below.

- Log in to your Gmail Account
- Click on the Google Drive icon from the 3x3 Application Launcher
- Click on "new" in your Google Drive
- Mouse on "Google Doc" from the dropdown menu

- Then, click on "Blank document" or "From a template" to create  a new Doc as  shown below.

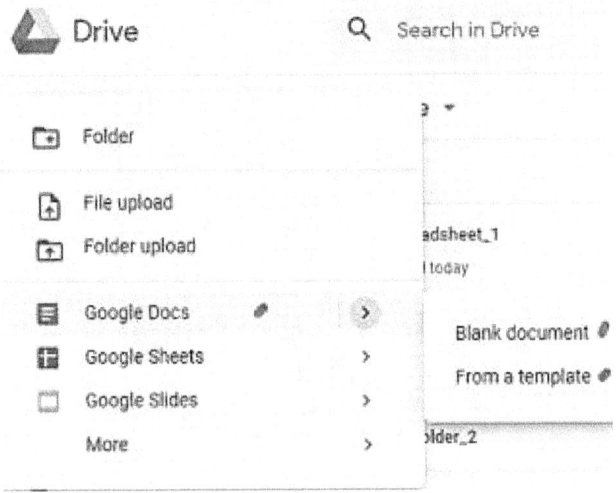

You can  also access  Google Drive when  you open your Gmail  and then click  directly on "Google Doc" in  a 3x3 Application  launcher.

# Creating a new Document in Docs

There are  a couple of ways by  which you can  create a new document  in Google Docs.

- Click  on "new" in your  Google Drive
- Mouse over "Google Doc" from the dropdown menu
- Then, click on "Blank document" or "From a template" to create a new Doc.

# Creating a new document in specific Folder

To create a new document in a particular folder, follow the steps below

- Double-click on the Folder where you want to create a new document to open it in My Drive
- Click on "New"
- Mouse over "Google Doc" and then select "Blank document" or "From template."

# Renaming your Document in Google Docs

To rename an existing file in Google Docs, follow the steps below.

- Right-click on the file and select "Rename" from the dropdown list
- Enter the new name in the dialog box that appears
- Then, click on "OK."

# Navigating Google Docs Interface

To use Google Docs most effectively, you need to understand the clickable buttons and menus in the Google Docs interface which are highlighted in the figure below.

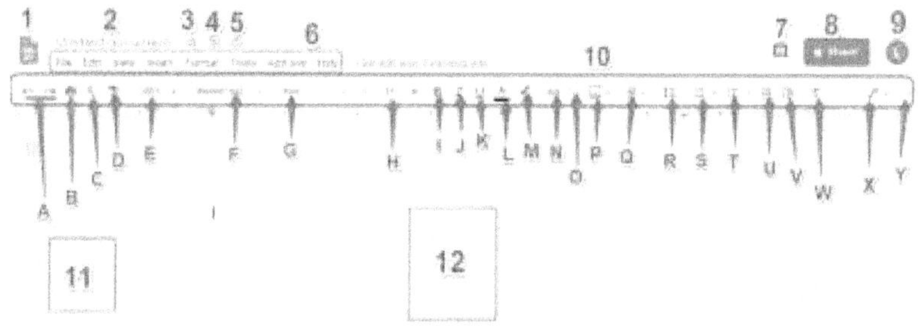


1. **Docs Home Screen**: This will migrate you to the Google Docs Home page where you have all your documents when you click on it.

2. **Document Title**: Document title enables you to rename your  document

3. **Star**: When  star is added  to a document, you will be able to find the document easily in Google Drive.

4. **Move Document**: This is a folder icon through which you can move the document to another folder or  location in your  Google Drive.

5. **See Document Status**: This enables you to  know the status  of your document. For  instance, you will know if changes you made to your document have been saves.

6. **Menu Bar**: This contains menus and submenus that are used for some specific functions in Google Docs. These include:

**File:** Here, we  have actions related  to file. You can  share the file, open a new file, download file, check version history  of a file, publish  a file to  web, etc.

**Edit:** This contains some  editing options such  as undo, redo, cut, copy, paste, delete  and so on.

**View:** This menu enables you to view and control how the document looks like on the screen. The sub menus in this category include: print layout, show ruler, mode, show document outline and show section break.

**Insert:** You can insert images, tables, drawings, charts, mathematical equations, and so on into your document.

**Format:** You can format your document to your taste with the aid of this powerful menu. The options available here include: text formatting, paragraph styles, align & indent, line spacing, bullet & numbering etc.

**Tools:** This menu contains some useful tools needed to work on your document. This include: spelling and grammar to check and correct spellings and grammar, word count to know the number of words contained in a document etc.

**Add-ons:** You can add additional functionalities to your Google Docs with this.

**Help:** You can get updates, training, privacy policy and terms of service here.

7. **Comment History**: This enables you to view comments on  your document  from collaborators.

8. **Share**: You can  share your  document with  other collaborators  by tapping on  the share icon.

9. **Google Account**: This  shows the  Google Account associated  with the Google Docs

10. **Toolbar**:  Toolbar  contains  clickable  icons  and buttons  which are used  to perform quick  actions on your  document. These include:

    A. Redo/undo: Undo  button  reverses  whatever you do while  redo will do what  you undo.

    B. Print: This is  used to print your  document

    C. Spelling  Check: This  is  used  to  check  and effect  the  correctness  of  spellings  and grammar  in your document

    D. Pain  format:  This  enables  you  to  use  the format  of  a  given  text  on  another  text without  going through a  long process.

    To use pain  format, highlight the  text you want to  use  the  format  and  click  on  the  pain format button. Now, highlight  your text and click on  the pain format  icon. The text  will be formatted  to the new format  you want.

E. **Zoom**: This is  used to change the zoom effect.

F. **Text Style**: This  enables  you  to  change  the style to  either heading  or style

G. **Font Type**: This  enables  you  to  change  the font type  of your document.

H. **Font Size**: This is  used to change  the font size of the text

I.  **Bold**: This  enable you to bold  your text

J. **Italic**: This enable  you to italicize  your text

K. **Underline**: This  enable you to  underline your text

L. **Text Colour**: This is  used  to  change  the font colour  of your text

M.  **Highlight Colour**: This  enables you to change the  colour behind  the text

N. **Insert Link**: This is used  to insert hyperlinks

O. **Add Comment**: This  enable authorized person to  add comments  to a document

P. **Insert Image**: This enables  you to insert image into  your document

Q. **Align**: This is used  to make text  alignment.

R. **Line Spacing**: This enables  you to modify  line spacing of  text in your  document.

S. **Numbered List**: This is used to insert numbered list  in document

T. **Bulleted  List**: This  is  used  to  insert  bulleted list in document

U. **Decrease Indent**: This is  used to decrease  the indentation.

V. **Increase  Indent**: This is  used to increase  the indentation

W.  **Clear  Formatting**: This  is  used  to  clear  all formatting in  a text and return  it to its default formatting  style.

X. **Collaboration Mode**: This  indicates the mode of  collaboration on a  document which  could be: **editing, suggesting** or  **viewing mode**.

Y. **Hide Menu**: This arrow  hides the menu  icons when you  click on it.

11. **Document Outline**: Headings  added to a document appear  here.

12. **Working Area**: This is  where the contents  of your document  go.

## How to attach a document to an email

To send  a Google Doc as  an attachment, follow  the steps bellow.

- Open  the  document  you  want  to  attach  to  an email in  Google Docs
- Click  on "File" on the  menu bar
- Scroll  down  and  mouse  over  "email"  from  the dropdown  menu.

- Then, select "Email this file"
- A box  appears. Click  on "attach" to select the File format
- Insert  the  email  addresses  of  the  recipients  and tap "Send"

# How to import a document in Google Drive

You can import files or folders into your Google Drive by either drag and drop method or by using "New" in Google Drive.

To import by Drag and Drop method,

- Click on the file or folder.
- Drag and Drop the file or folder in Google Drive window

To import by using "New",

- Open your Google Drive
- Click on "New"

- Click on "File upload" or "Folder upload" as the case may be

- A browser  window appears

- Locate  your file or folder  and select your  file or folder

- Click on "Open" in the  case of file while you  click on "Upload" in the  case of  a folder.

## How to Export Document in Google Drive

To take  a file you created  in Google Drive to  another format,

- Double-click on  the file

- Click on  the "File" option on the  menu bar

- Mouse  over "download in" and Select  your desired format

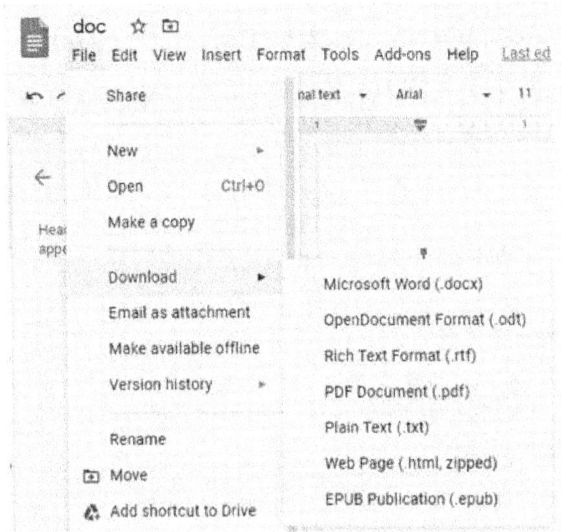

- Open the file from your download and enable editing.

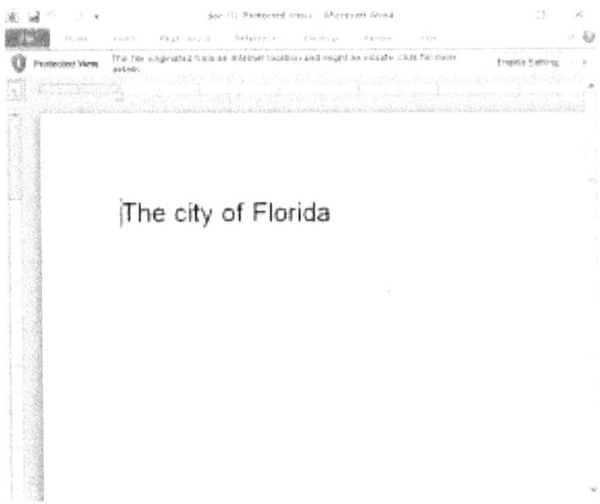

# Navigating the Blank Drawing Canvas

Tools are available in Google Drawing to make charts and  drawings. Some of these  tools are highlighted in  the figure below.

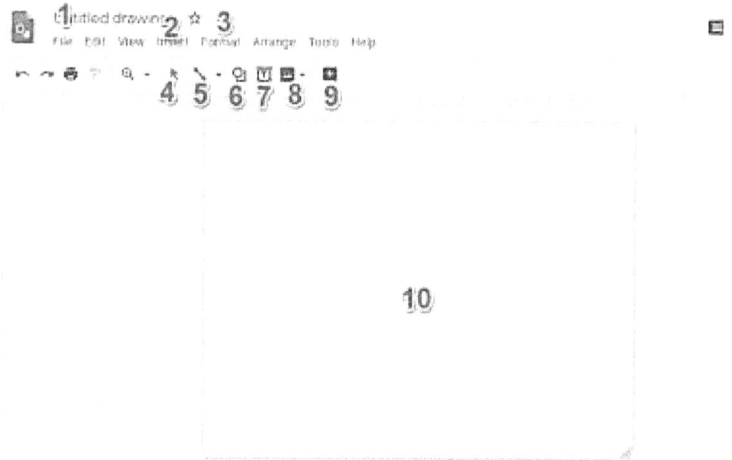

1. **File**: File has some commands to share your drawing  with other  people, create a new  drawing, document, spreadsheet, publish  your drawing file in web  and open existing drawing files among others.

2. **Insert**: This enables you to insert images, text boxes,     shapes,     tables,     and charts     into your  drawing.

3. **Format**: The format menu allows you to format text in your drawing like line spacing, align and indent, inserting bullets and numbering, add tables, fill color, and many more.

4. **Select**: This enables you to select an object in the drawing area. An object could be a single line segment, a shape, or a free picture.

5. **Select line**: This is where you select lines to make your drawings which include: line, arrow, elbow connector, curved connector, curve, polyline and Scribble

6. **Shape tool**: This contains some different shapes that you can use to make charts and diagrams.

7. **Text box**: Text box enables you to insert text boxes in the drawing area to enter text into your drawing.

8. **Image tool**: This enables you to upload images from your computer, web, photos, and more into your drawing.

9. **Add comment**: This enables you to add comments to your drawing file.

10. **Drawing area**: This is the region where you make your charts and diagrams.

# Chapter 2

# Adding & Editing Text in Google Docs

# Inserting Text box

To insert a text box:

- Open your document and tap on "Insert" on the menu bar

- Mouse over "Drawing" from the dropdown menu and click on "**+New**." A text area with a tool bar appears

- Click on the Text box on the tool bar

- Left-click the text area, hold and drag the mouse in the text area

- Release the mouse and a text box appears

- Enter your text inside the box and click "Save and close"

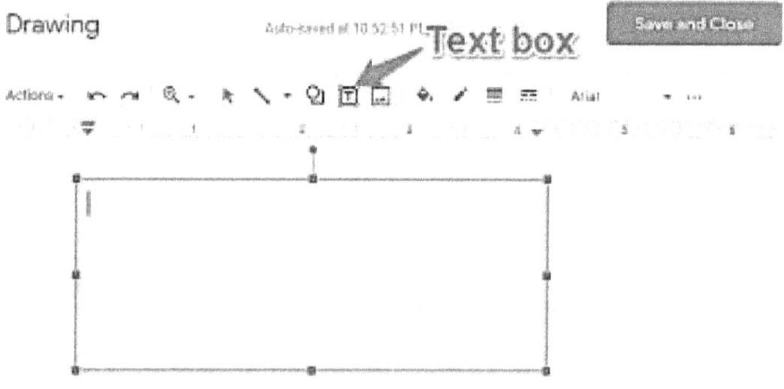

# How to select Text

To select text:

- Position your cursor at the beginning or end of the text
- Left-click and mouse over the text

Alternatively, you can use short cut button to select all text by pressing "**ctrl + A**"

# How to change Text Font

To change the font of a text: Select the text and click "Font" in the toolbar. Then, select the font of your choice.

# Adding more font

You can  use the font  menu to add more  fonts to the Google Docs. To  do this:

- Open  your document in  Google Docs
- Click on  font menu and  tap on "More  font" from the drop-down  menu. The font  dialog box appears.
- Select  fonts you  wish  to add and  click "OK." The fonts will  be added to your  font main list

# Changing Font size

To change  the font size  of text:

- Select the  text and tap on  font size on the  toolbar
- Select a  font size or  enter your desired font  size and tap "Enter key" on  your device. You  can also

increase/decrease the font size by tapping on the "+/-" signs.

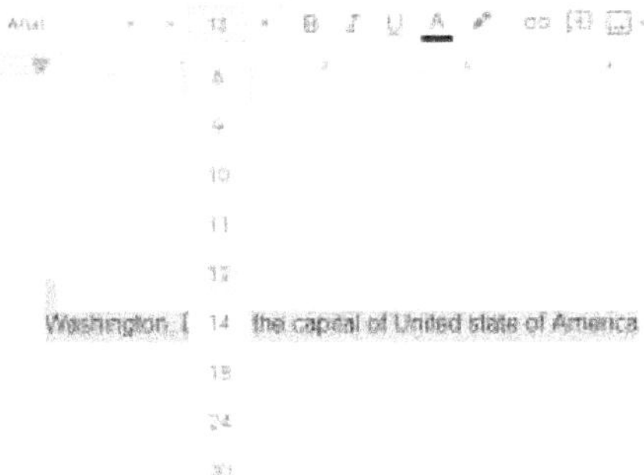

## How to Bold, Italicize & Underline Text

To add bold, italic or underline to a text, select the text and tap on bold, italic or underline from the toolbar.

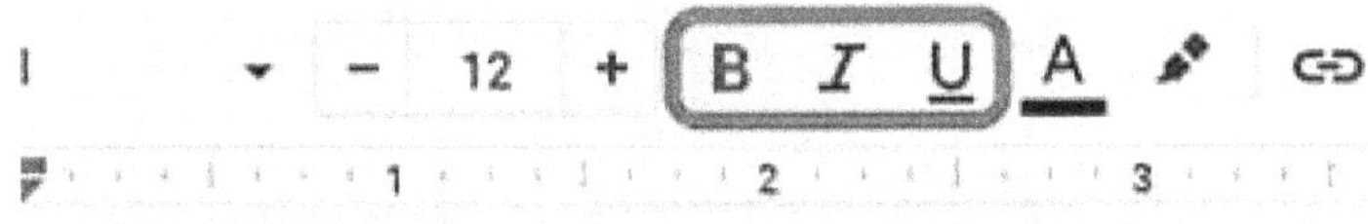

**Washington, D.C is the capital of United state**

# Changing the Text Font Colour

- Select the text you wish to modify and click Text colour icon from the toolbar. A drop-down menu of text colours appears.

- Select the colour of your choice. The text colour will change to the selected colour.

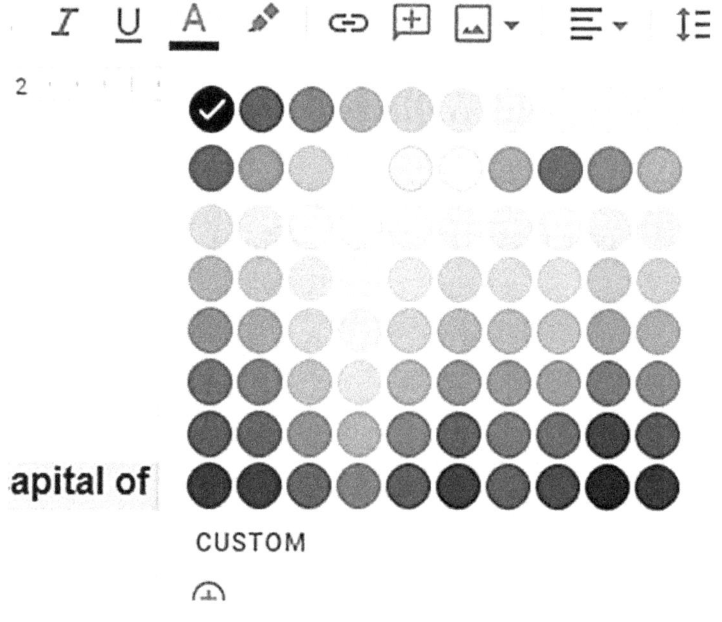

# Adding Stroke through a Text

Strikethrough is a horizontal line draw through text to indicate the removal of the text in a draft. To strike-through a text:

- Select the  text and tap  on "Format" on  the menu bar

- Hover  on  the  "Text"  from  the  drop-down  menu and tap  on "Strikethrough"

Format   Tools   Add-ons   Help      Last edit was seconds ago

| Text | ▸ | B | Bold | Ctrl+B |
| Paragraph styles | ▸ | $I$ | Italic | Ctrl+I |
| Align & indent | ▸ | U | Underline | Ctrl+U |
| Line spacing | ▸ | S | Strikethrough | Alt+Shift+5 |
| Columns | ▸ | X' | Superscript | Ctrl+. |
| Bullets & numbering | ▸ | X₂ | Subscript | Ctrl+, |

Alternatively, you can strikethrough your text by using shortcut. Select the text and press **"Alt + Shift +5"** simultaneously.

# Adding Superscript & Subscript

To format  a text with superscript  or subscript:

- Open the  document and  position the cursor where you  want to insert  the "superscript" or "subscript"

- Tap  on "Format" on the  menu bar

- Hover  on "Text" on the  drop-down menu

- Select  "superscript"  or  "subscript"  from  the  sub-menu

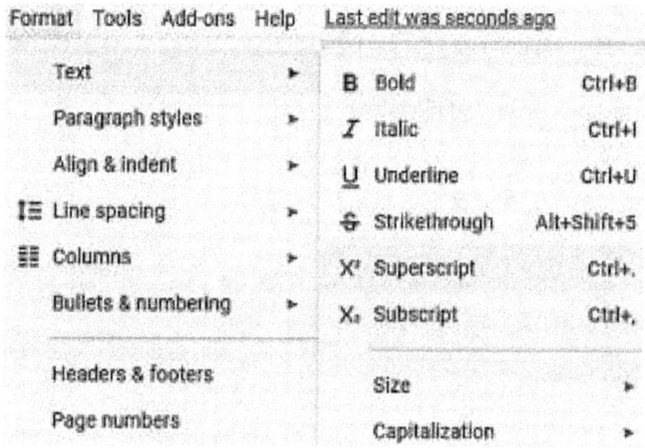

- Enter  your  text  which  now  appears  as  super-script/subscript

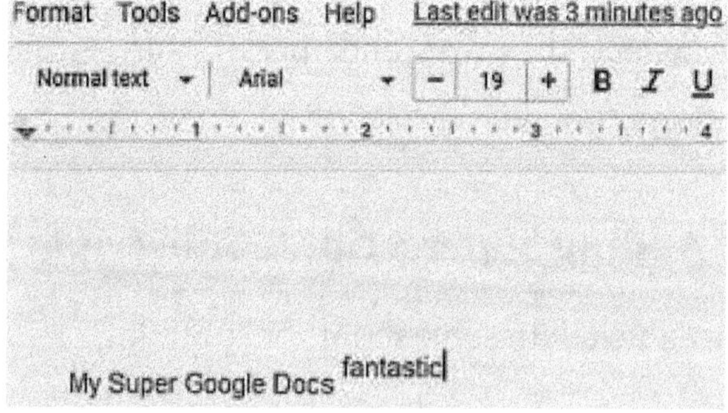

Alternatively, you can press "**Ctrl +.**" or "**Ctrl +,**" for superscript and subscript respectively after you have positioned the cursor where you want the super-script/subscript.

You can also use the special character insertion tool built-in Google Docs to insert superscript/subscript in your document. To do this, follow the steps below:

- Open your document in Google Docs
- Position your cursor where you want the superscript/subscript inserted
- Tap on "Insert" on the menu bar
- Scroll down and tap on "Special Characters" from the drop-down list
- Tap on the arrow-down button and select Superscript/subscript

# Chapter 3

# Working with Tables in Google Docs

# How to insert Table

A table is a grid of cells arranged in rows and columns. Tables are used to organize and present text information and numerical values. To insert a table:

- Open your document in Google Docs and position the insertion point where you want the table

- Tap on the "Insert" menu on the menu bar, scroll down and mouse over "Table." A grid of squares appears.

- Drag the mouse over the grid of squares to select the number of cells(i.e rows and columns) to make your table.

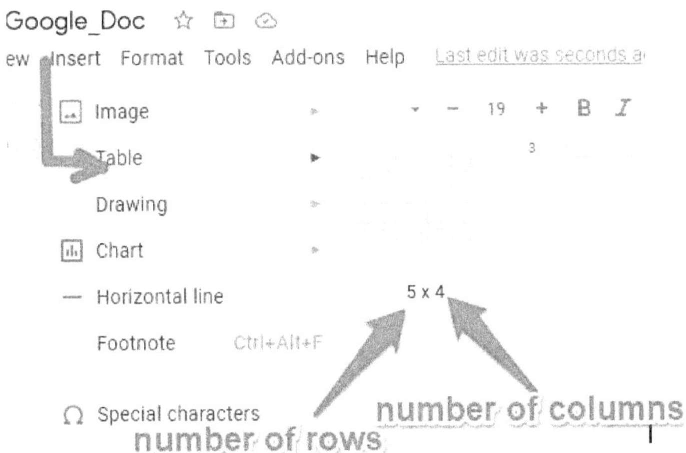

- Click the mouse, and the table appears in the document with the insertion point in the first cell

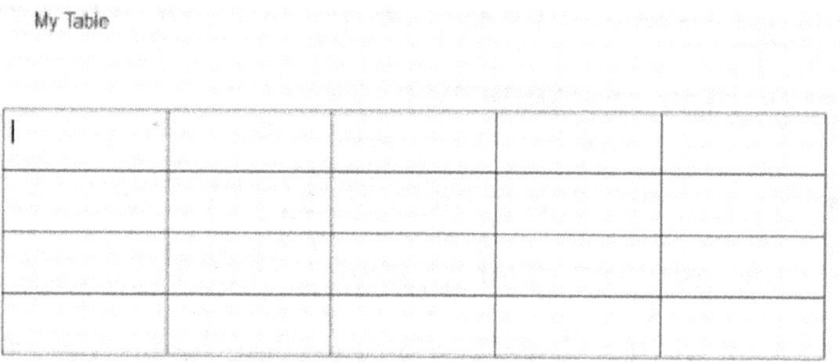



# Adding Data to a Table

To add data to a table:

- Click on the cell to position the insertion point there

- Enter your data in the cell

- Move the insertion point to other cell

| Monday | Tuesday | Wednesday | Thursday | Friday |
|--------|---------|-----------|----------|--------|
| 20 | 25 | 15 | 22 | 41 |
| 35 | 28 | 12 | 54 | 50 |
| 18 | 32 | 23 | 37 | 48 |

# Inserting Rows and Columns

To insert an additional row in your table:

- Right-click a cell in the row adjacent to the location where you want to insert the row

- Then, select "Insert row above" or "insert row below" from the dropdown menu that appears

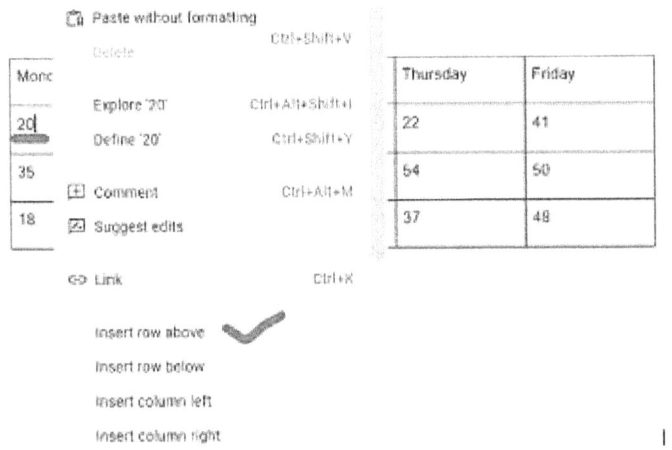


- A new row appears in the table

| Monday | Tuesday | Wednesday | Thursday | Friday |
|--------|---------|-----------|----------|--------|
|  |  |  |  |  |
| 20 | 25 | 15 | 22 | 41 |
| 35 | 28 | 12 | 54 | 50 |
| 18 | 32 | 23 | 37 | 48 |

To insert an additional column in a table:

- Right-click a cell in the column adjacent to the location  where you want  to insert the  column

- Then, select "Insert column left" or "insert column right" from the  dropdown menu  that appears.

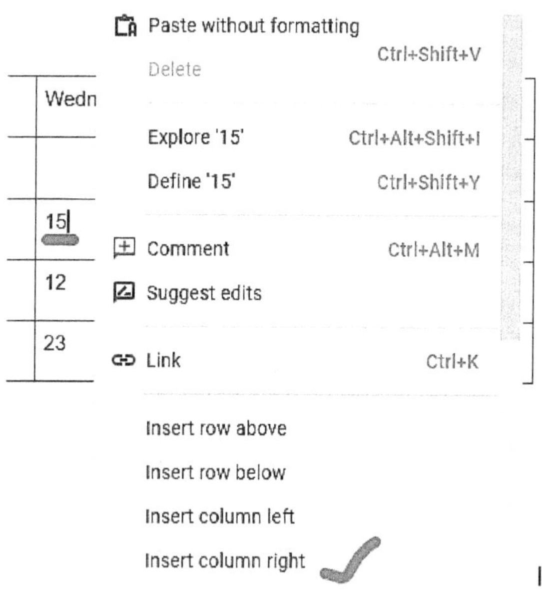


- A new  column appears  in the table

| Monday | Tuesday | Wednesday | | Thursday | Friday |
|---|---|---|---|---|---|
|  |  |  |  |  |  |
| 20 | 25 | 15 |  | 22 | 41 |
| 35 | 28 | 12 |  | 54 | 50 |
| 18 | 32 | 23 |  | 37 | 48 |

# Deleting Row or Column

To get rid  of a row or colun  in a table:

- Right-click  on a cell in  the row or column  you want to delete.

- Then, select "Delete row" or "Delete column" from the drop-down  menu that  appears.

| Monday | Tuesday | Wed |
|--------|---------|-----|
| 20 | 25 | 15 |
| 35 | 28 | 12 |
| 18 | 32 | 23 |

Insert column left

Insert column right

Delete row

Delete column

Delete table

Distribute rows

# Deleting a Table

To delete  a table from  your  document, right-click  on a cell in the  table and tap  on "Delete table" from the  drop-down menu  that appears

| Monday | Tuesday |
| --- | --- |
| 20 | 25 |
| 35 | 28 |
| 18 | 32 |

Insert column left

Insert column right

Delete row

Delete column

Delete table ✓

Distribute rows

# Distribute Row and Column

Row or column distribution is the spacing of table rows and columns evenly. To distribute row or column:

- Highlight the rows or columns that you want to distribute

- Right-click on the grey area and select "Distribute rows" or "Distribute columns" from the drop-down menu that appears.

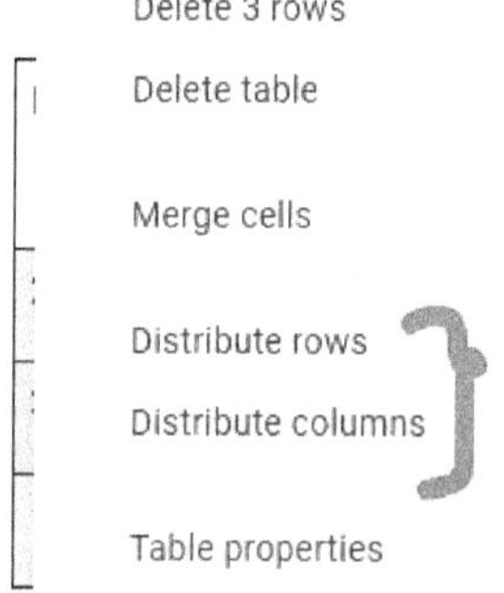


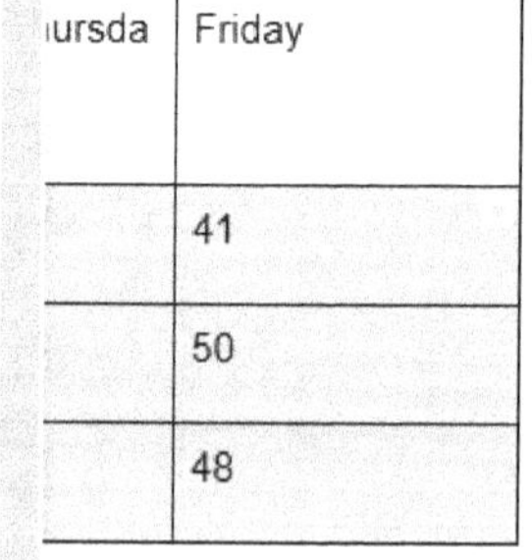

# Merging and Unmerging Rows  & Coloumns

To merge rows or columns:

- Click and  drag your  mouse over the  cells you want to merge  to highlight  them

- Right-click  on  the  selected  cells.  A  drop-down menu  appears

- Scroll  down the menu  and tap on "Merge cell"

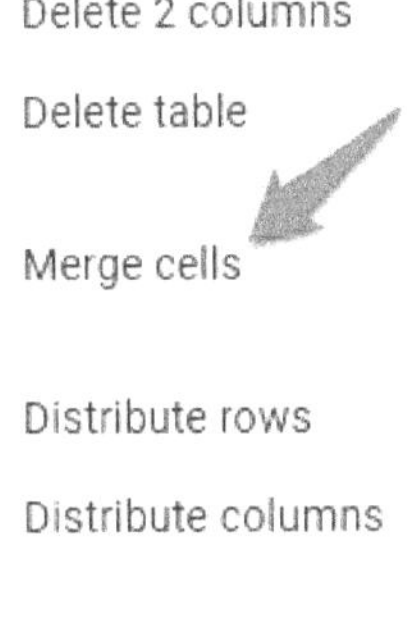



| | Monday | Tuesda |
|---|---|---|
| | 20 | 25 |
| | 35 | 28 |
| | 18 | 32 |

- The selected  cells are  merged together

| Monday | | | | |
|---|---|---|---|---|
| Tuesday | Wednesday | Thursday | Friday | |
| 20 | 25 | 15 | 22 | 41 |
| 35 | 28 | 12 | 54 | 50 |
| 18 | 32 | 23 | 37 | 48 |

# Alignment of Cells in a Table

Vertical cells alignment and horizontal cells alignment are done to reposition cell contents in a table. In vertical cell alignment, cell contents can be aligned to the top, middle, or bottom area of the cell while cell contents can be aligned to the left, center, or right side of the cell in horizontal cells alignment.

To enable vertical cell alignment,

- Select the cell or cells you want to align.
- Right-click and tap on "Table properties" from the drop-down menu that appears
- Click on "Vertical alignment" from the Table Properties Dialog box that appears.
- Select your desired alignment and click "OK"

To enable horizontal cells alignment;

- Select the cell or cells you want to align.
- Click on your desired alignment button from the four options in the shortcut toolbar

- The text  will be  realigned

## Modifying Table Borders

When working with tables in Google Docs , you can change the styles and color of the table borders. To modify table borders, right-click on the table. Scroll-down the drop-down menu and click on "Table properties." A table properties window appears where you can change the size and color of the borders as shown below.

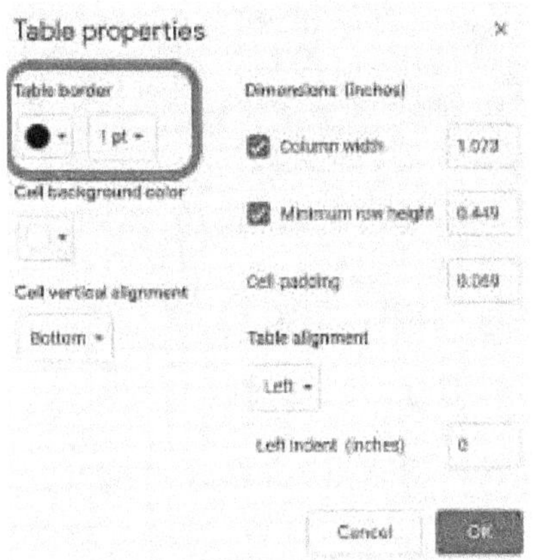

## Modifying Specific Table Borders

To modify a specific border in a table, click on each borders individually. A new short cut menu appears on top of the document. Then, modify the thickness, color and style  of the selected  border.

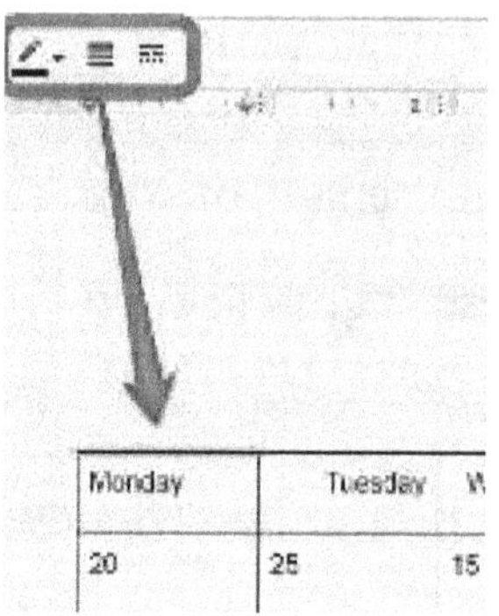

# Table Alignment

To change the vertical alignment of cell(s) in Google Docs, follow  the steps below.

- Open  your document in  Google Docs
- Select  the cell(s) you  wish to modify
- Right-click on the table cells and select "Table Properties" from  the dropdown menu
- Select "Cell Vertical alignment"
- Select your desired veretical alignment and click "OK"

# Changing Cell backgroung colour

To change  cell colour  background:

- Select  the cell or cells  that you want to  modify
- Right-click  and  select  "Table  properties"  from  the menu that  appears.

| | Monday | Tuesday | Wedn |
|---|---|---|---|
| 20 | 25 | 15 |
| 35 | 28 | 12 |
| 18 | 32 | 23 |

Delete row

Delete table

Merge cells

Distribute rows

Distribute columns

Table properties

- The  Table  properties  dialog  box  appears.  Click  on the "Cell background colour" drop-down  arrow
- Select your  desired colour  from the grid  of colours that appears  and click "OK"

Table properties     ×

Table border

● ▾   1 pt ▾

Cell background color

⬚ None

CUSTOM

Dimensions (inches)

☑ Column width    1.073

☐ Minimum row height

ding    0.069

gnment

lent (inches)    0

Cancel    OK

# Chapter 4

# Images, page numbers & graph

# Inserting Images

Documents become more visually appealing when images are added. Images can be added to a text from a computer, web, Drive, Photos, URL, or Camera.

To add an image from your computer, follow the steps below.

- Open your document and place the cursor where you want the image on the document.
- Click on the image menu on the toolbar.
- You are prompted to upload the image.
- Select "Upload from computer."

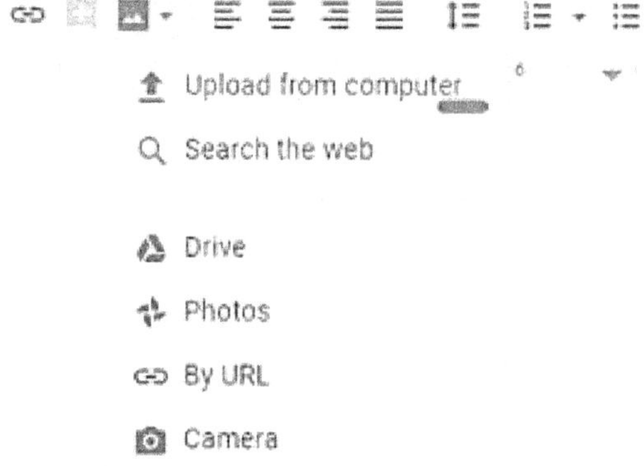


- Locate your image file on your computer
- Select the picture and tap on "Open."

To add an image from the URL:

- Open your document and place the cursor where you want the image on the document

- Click on the image menu on the toolbar

- Select "By URL"

- A dialog box appears. Enter the image address then, click on "insert."

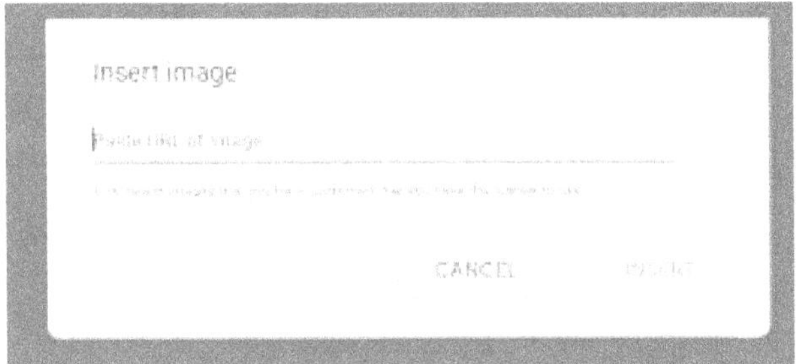

## Resizing the Image

To resize an image, select the image. Resizing handles appear around the selected image.

Click and  drag one of  the resizing handles  at the corners. The  image  is  resized  proportionately.  The  side  resizing  handles  are  used  to  stretch  the  image  vertically  or  horizontally

## Cropping an Image

To  crop  an  image,  select  the  image,  right-click  on  the  selected  image, and click "Crop" from  the drop-down menu. Adjustable  handles appear  around the image.

When  you  are  satisfied,  press  "Enter"  on  your  keyboard/ click anywhere  in your file.

# Rotating an Image

To rotate an image, open the document containing the image in Google Docs:

- Click the  mage you want to rotate. Eight blue dots will appear around the image borders out of which one will have extra dot connected to it.

- Hover on this dot and your cursor will change to a crosshair.

- Click and drag the dot to rotate the picture to your desired degree of orientation through the displayed rotation degree.

# Changing Image Properties

You can change the image properties like colour, transparency, brightness and more. To do this, right-click on the image and select "Image options" from the drop-down menu. The "Image option" side toolbar will appear. Click on any of the options available to access and change the image properties.

> **Image options**   ✕

> Size & Rotation

> Text Wrapping

> Position

> Recolor

> Adjustments

# How to reset and replace an Image

If you  have an image  that you have edited in  Google Docs and  you  aren't  satisfied,  you  can  revert  to  its  original status  rather than undoing  each step. To  do  this, right-click on  the image and  click "Reset image" from  the drop-down  menu. The  image  will  be  restored  to  its  original status.

If you  are satisfied with  the formatting of  an image but you want  to replace the  image, right-click  on the image and  select  "Replace Image"  from  the  drop-down  menu. The image  will be replaced  with the previous  formatting maintained. To  do this, right-click  on the image  and click "Replace image" from the drop-down menu.

# Positioning image in Text

To change  the position of an  image from one  location to another in  a  document  is  difficult.  This  is  due  to  text wrapping  settings  on  the  image.  To  move  the  image freely, text  wrapping settings  have to be  changed. There are three  positions available. These are:

- **In line**: Image is aligned with the text. The image moves with the text if additional text is added or deleted.

- **Wrap text**: Text is wrapped around the image. This option is good when you want to move image from one location to another in a document.

- **Break text**: This option is similar to text wrapping but the text will appear above and below the image.

To edit the position of an image, select the image. The three position options appear below the image.

Select "wrap text." Left-click and drag the image to your desired location.

# Inserting graph in your document

You can generate graph from a table in your Google Docs. To do this, highlight all the cells in the table.

- Click "Insert" on the menu bar

- Select "Chart" from the drop-down menu and tap "Line"

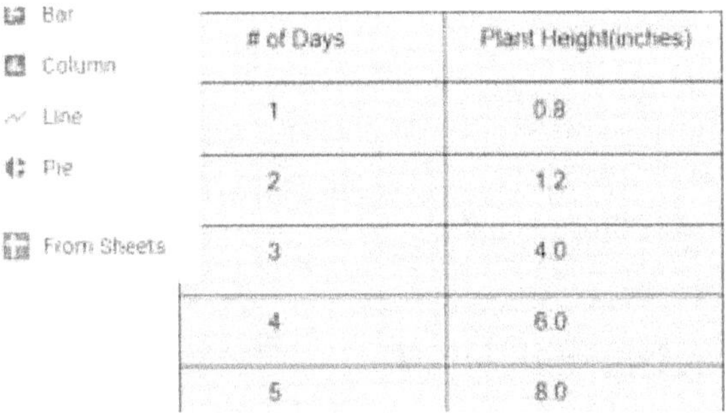

Bar

Column

Line

Pie

From Sheets

| # of Days | Plant Height(inches) |
| --- | --- |
| 1 | 0.8 |
| 2 | 1.2 |
| 3 | 4.0 |
| 4 | 6.0 |
| 5 | 8.0 |

- The table is converted into a line graph as shown below.

# Chapter 5

# Making Bullet & Number Lists

# How to add bullet list

To add  bullet, click bullet  list button from  the toolbar

- Next, type  the first item  and press "Enter" and the cursor  moves to the  next line.
- If the  items are already  typed, highlight  the items

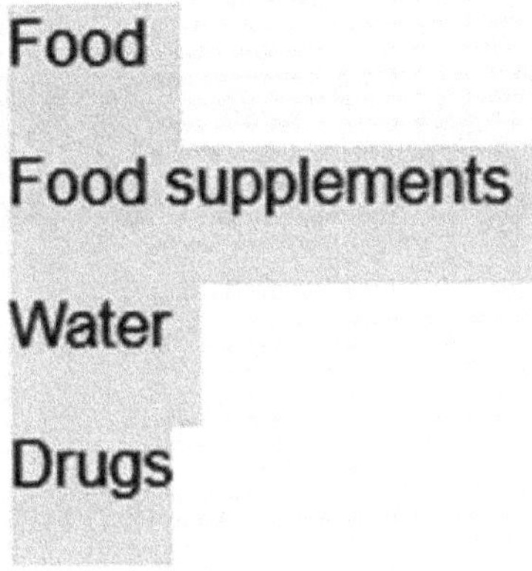


- Next, click  bulleted list  icon on the  toolbar

- Food

- Food supplements

- Water

- Drugs

## How to add Numbered List

To add numbered list, click numbered list button on the toolbar.

- Next, type the first item and press "Enter" and the cursor moves to the next line.

- If the items are already typed, highlight the items

- Next, click numbered list icon on the toolbar

1. Food

2. Food supplements

3. Water

4. Drugs

# How to create Multilevel List

To create  a multilevel list, click "numbered list" button on the  toolbar and click  the arrow beside  the button. A list of multilevel  list pattern  appears.

- Select  your desired  pattern
- Enter the  first item and  press enter

- Next, press "Tab" on  your keyboard  to enter lower level.

1. Food
   - Rice
   - Yam
   - 

- Next, press "Shift Tab" to  return to higher  list level and enter  the next item

1. Food
   - Rice
   - Yam
2. Food supplement

# Chapter 6

# Advanced Formatting and Page setup

# Editing Line Spacing

When you increase the line spacing of text in your document, readability is improved. To change the line spacing, highlight the content and click "Format" in the toolbar. Then, mouse over "Line spacing" in the drop-down menu  and select your desired  line spacing.

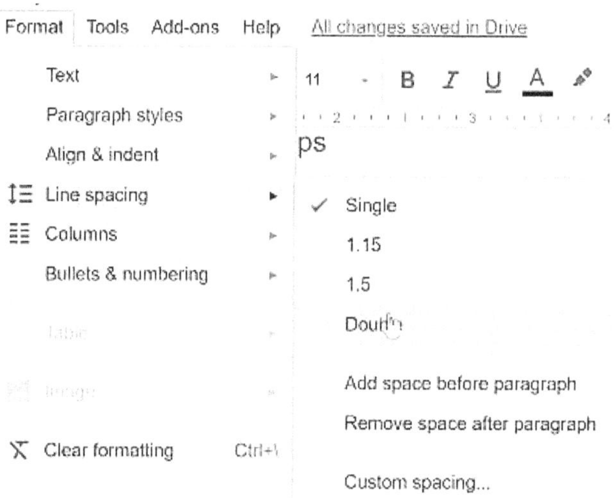

To have  more control  of customizing line  spacing, click on "Custom spacing" as shown above.

Custom spacing

**Line spacing**       **Paragraph spacing** (pts)

1.14                   Before    0

                       After     20

Apply          Cancel

# Column Setting

If you  want the contents  of your document  to be in columns, highlight  the content you  want to take to columns.

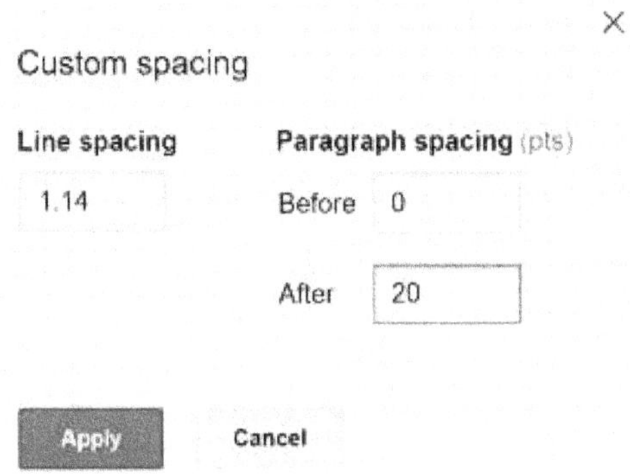



- Click "Format" in the  toolbar.

- Mouse  over "Columns" from the  drop-down menu

- Select  the  column  pattern  from  the  options  that  pop up

If you have an image that you have edited in Google Docs and you aren't satisfied, you can revert to its original status rather than undoing each step. To do this, right-click on the image and click "Reset image" from the drop-down menu. The image will be restored to its original status.

If you are satisfied with the formatting of an image but you want to replace the image, right-click on the image and select "Replace image" in the drop-down menu. The image will be replaced while the previous format is maintained. To do this, right-click on the image and click "Replace image" from the drop-down menu.

To add  line in between  the columns, change  the numbers of column,

- Select the contents and click "Format" in the toolbar
- Mouse  over  "Columns"  in  the  drop-down  menu and  click "more option"

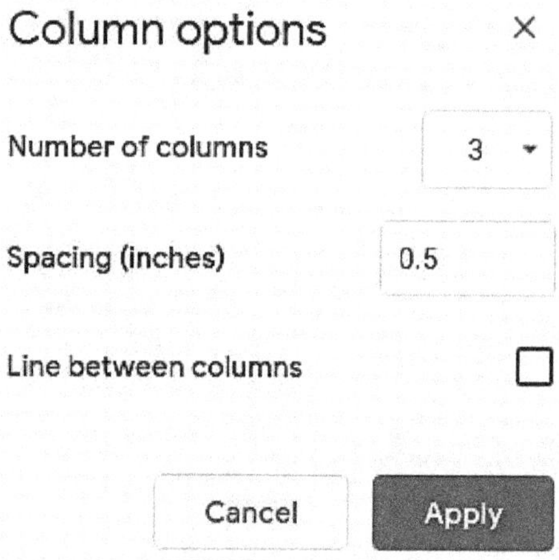

# Adding Page Numbers

To insert page number,

- Open your document and tap on "Insert"
- Scroll down and mouse over page number
- Then, select the format of your interest

# Inserting Headers &Footers

To insert headers and footers,

- Open the document and tap on "Insert" on the menu bar
- Scroll down, mouse over "Headers & Footers" and tap on "Header" or "Footer"

- Then, enter header in the typing area and click "Enter"

# How to Format Header & Footer

You can  adjust the headers  and footers margins  of your document. To do this,

- Open  the  document  in  Google  Docs  and  click "Format" on  the menu bar
- Tap  on  Headers  &  Footers  from  the  drop-down menu. A  dialog box  appears.

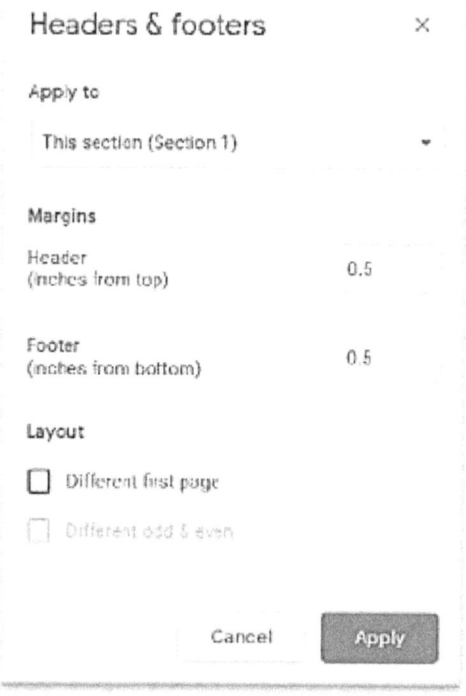


- Enter your  desired margin  size and tap "Apply"

# Adding a Foot Note to Document

- Open your  document in  Google Docs

- Position  your insertion  point where you  want the foot note

- Tap  on "Insert" on the  menu bar

- Scroll  down and  tap "Foot Note"

- Type your  Foot note and  press "Enter"

# Editing Page Setup

You can  make page setup  changes to your  document in Google  Docs just  like any  other  word processing application.  Page  setup  properties  include:  orientation, paper size, page  colour and  margin.

- To make  page setup  changes,

- Open your  document in  Google Docs

- Click  "File" in  the  toolbar,  scroll  down  the  drop-down  menu and tap  on "Page setup." A page setup dialog  box will appear.

- Edit  the page setup  and click "OK"

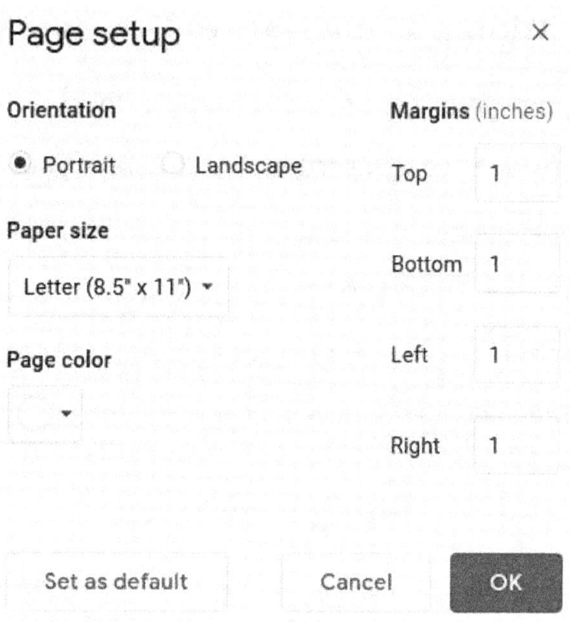
Page setup
X
Orientation
Portrait     Landscape
Paper size
Letter (8.5" x 11")
Page color
Margins (inches)
Top        1
Bottom     1
Left       1
Right      1
Set as default     Cancel     OK

# Chapter 7

## Paragraph Styles in Google Docs

## Understanding Paragraph styles

A document may comprises of title, main heading, sub-headings and body text. All these are styled differently to give the document a structure. Meanwhile, working with large document could be challenging as regards ensuring there is consistent style to it. Paragraph styles enable us to maintain consistent styles and allow us to make changes that affect the whole text in our document quickly and easily. In Google Docs, Paragraph style is made up of different components which include: Normal text, Title, Subtitle, Heading 1, Heading 2 to Heading 6. All these components are styled differently and used for different components of a document to make a good document structure.

## How to select a paragraph

Click and drag your mouse from the beginning of the first sentence to the end of the last sentence or simply triple-click anywhere in the paragraph to select all the content of the paragraph.

# Setting a Paragraph Style

To use paragraph style,

- Select the text you want to apply style to and change the font, font size, colour, e.t.c to your taste  using the formatting  tools on the toolbar.

# Cropping an Image

- Click "Format" on  the toolbar and  Hover on "Paragraph Styles" from the  drop-down menu.
- Hover  on "Heading 2" and select "Update 'Heading 2' to match

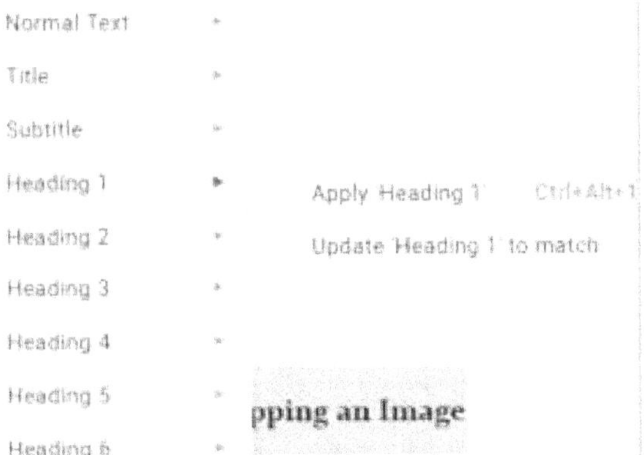

This will automatically change all the Heading 2 text in the document to the paragraph style.

## Borders & Shading

To add a border around the page,

- Open your document in Google Docs and click "Insert" in the menu bar
- Hover your cursor on "Table" in the drop-down menu. The table size selection pops up to the right
- Select and click 1x1 grid
- Resize the table to fit in your document

To add border around a paragraph,

- Open the document in Google Docs
- Click to position your cursor inside the paragraph
- Click "Format" on the menu bar
- Hover on "Paragraph Styles" and click "Borders and Shading" in the sub-menu.

# Outline

The outline tool in Google Docs makes navigating through a lengthy document much easy in a single click. Though, Google Docs will automatically add headings to an outline but you can also add them manually.

To do this,

- Open your document in Google Docs

- Select the text you want to make a heading.

- Click "Format" on the menu bar and hover on "Paragraph Styles" from the drop-down menu.

- Hover on "Heading **x**" and select "Update "Heading **x**" to match

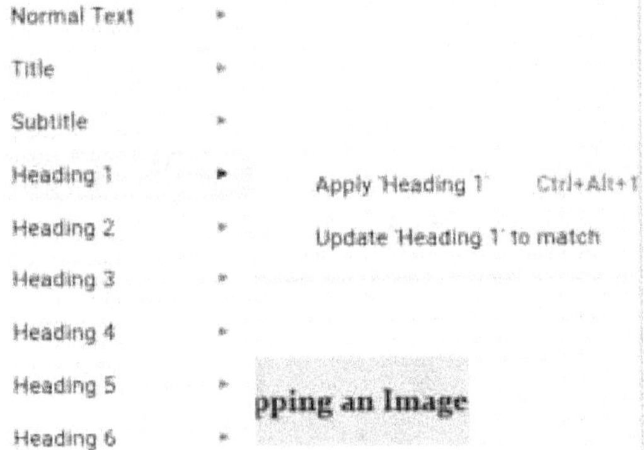


- The text appears on the outline window

# Chapter 8

# Inserting Lines, Drawings & Hyperlinks

# **Inserting Hyperlinks**

A hyperlink is a text or image that can be clicked to migrate to a new document in outside websites or other G suite. To insert a hyperlink;

- Select the text you want to make a hyperlink

- Right-click on the selected text and tap "Link" from the drop-down menu. A dialog box appears.

- Enter the link (address) of the document you want to link to and tap "Apply."

To remove the link, click on the hyperlinked text and tap on "Remove"

# Inserting Drawings

You can insert a Google drawing into your Google Doc. Position the cursor where you want the drawing to go. Click "Insert" on the menu bar and tap "Drawing" from the drop-down menu and click "New." A drawing window appears.

Click the line tool and choose "Scribble." Make free hand drawing with scribble. Click "Save and close." The drawing is inserted where you want it.

You can also insert an existing drawing from your Google Drive. To do this, click "Insert" on the menu bar and tap "Drawing" from the drop-down menu and click "From Drive" from the sub-menu. The "Insert Drawing" window appears. Click on the drawing you want to use and click "Select." The drawing will be inserted in your drawing canvas.

## Inserting Lines

You can insert lines into your Google Docs by using Drawing Tools

- Position your cursor where you want the line on your document
- Click "Insert" on the toolbar
- Mouse over "Drawing" from the drop-down menu and tap "+New" from the sub-menu that appear. A checkered window with toolbar pops up
- Click on "Line Selection" from the toolbar and select your desired line from the list options

- Click  on "Save and Close" when  you are done.

# Chapter 9

# Voice Typing, Printing & Publishing of Documents

# Voice Typing in Google Docs

With Google Docs, using the keyboard isn't the only option to  add text. You  can also just talk  and have Google inscribe the  words for you  by using voice  typing. To use this feature, you  must use Google  Chrome web  browser and  your  computer  need  to  have  a  microphone.  Now, let's go.

- Open Google  Docs with Google  Chrome browser
- Open a  new /existing document  in Google docs
- Click  on  "Tools"  on  the  menu  bar.  A  dropdown menu appears
- Click on "Voice typing." A dialog  box appears.

- Click on  the microphone. If  a pop up  appears, click on "Allow" to enable Google access the microphone.

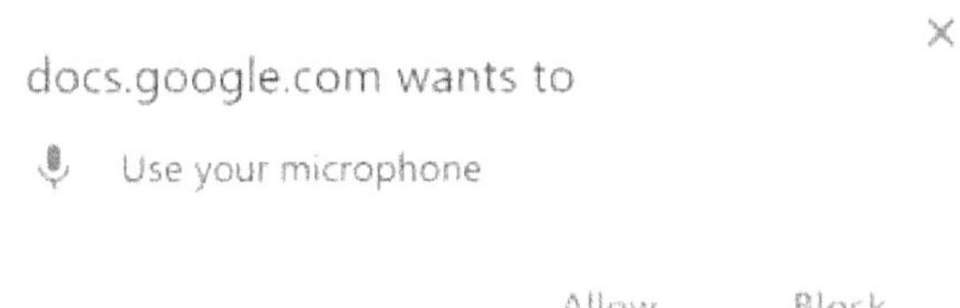


- Then, starts  speaking as soon  as the microphone's colour changes  from grey to red.

## How to publish file in Google Docs

When  you  publish  a  Google  Docs  file  to  the  web,  you create  a  copy of the file  as a separate  webpage with its own URL  through which  anyone can view the  content of the file. Publishing  enables you  to show your  document to a large  audience online. You  can link to or  embed your document.  When  you  embedded  your  document,  you make  the  document  available  for  view  in  an  existing website. To  publish your  document:

- Open the  file in Google  Docs
- Tap on "File" on the  menu bar

- Click  on "Publish to web" from  the drop-down list.
  A window appears.

- Click " Link/Embed" and  tap on "publishing"

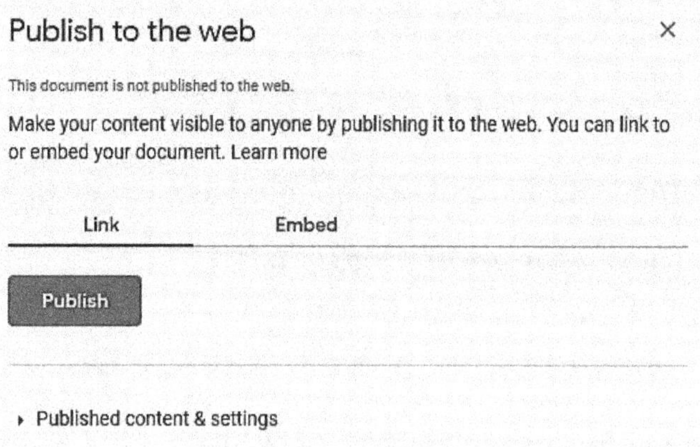



- A dialog  box appears  asking if you  want to publish
  the document.

- Click "OK"

For  Link, copy the URL  and send it to  anyone you would
like to  see the document  or share the URL  via Facebook,
Gmail or  Twitter.

For  Embed, copy the  HTML that appears  in the text box
and paste  it into your site  or blog.

# How to stop publishing a file

To remove  the file from  web, stop  publishing the  file. To stop  publishing  a file:

- Open  the file in  Google Docs
- Tap on "File" on  the menu bar
- Click  on "Publish to web" from  the drop-down list. A window appears.
- Click "Published  Content & Settings"
- Tap  on "Stop Publishing"

▾ Published content & settings

Stop publishing

☑ Automatically republish when changes are made

- A dialog box appears asking if you want to stop publishing the  document.
- Click "OK"

## How to print files in Google Docs

You can  print your documents  in Google Docs  though its complex  depending  on  your  browser  and  your  system configuration. To  print in Chrome, follow  the steps below:

- Open  the document you  want to print
- Click  on "File" from the  menu bar
- Scroll  down  and  tap  on  "Print."  A  dialog  box appears
- Click on  print button
- You  will  be  prompted  to  save  the  print  output. Enter the  file name and  click "Save"

- Open the  PDF file and  click the print  icon from the
  PDF viewer. Select  your printer and  click "Print"

www.ingramcontent.com/pod-product-compliance
Lightning Source LLC
Chambersburg PA
CBHW071940120726
48001CB00005B/1979